Along the

BLUE RIDGE PARKWAY

Photography by George Humphries
Historical text by Harley E. Jolley
Natural science text by J. Dan Pittillo

WESTCLIFFE PUBLISHERS

ENGLEWOOD, COLORADO

This book is dedicated with all
my love to my wife, Linda,
and my children,
Katie, Sean, and Weston.

Acknowledgments

*Thank you to the following people
for their love and commitment to
the Blue Ridge Parkway and for
helping to make this book a reality:
Bambi Teague (parkway biologist);
Phil Noblitt (parkway interpretation);
parkway rangers Lillian McElrath,
Marsha Bowers and Jimmy Haynes
(retired); parkway volunteers Bob
and Gussie Grey; Mrs. O'Connell
(Pisgah Inn); Thomas Lacy (Crabtree
Meadows); Karen Searle (Eastern
National); Barbara Allen and Jake
Messer (Switzerland General Store);
and my best friends Bill Duyck
and John Tingle.*

—G.H.

INTERNATIONAL STANDARD BOOK NUMBER: 1-56579-238-6 (HC), 1-56579-230-0 (SC)

PUBLISHER'S CATALOGING-IN-PUBLICATION

Humphries, George.
     Along the Blue Ridge Parkway / photography by George Humphries ;
     text by Harley E. Jolley and J. Dan Pittillo. — 1st ed.
       p. cm.
       ISBN 1-56579-238-6 (hc)
       1-56579-230-0 (sc)

     1. Blue Ridge Parkway (N.C. and Va.) 2. Blue Ridge Parkway
(N.C. and Va.)—Photographs.   I. Jolley, Harley E. II. Pittillo, J. Dan. III. Title.
     F217.B6H85 1997   975.5'0222
                                        QBI97-40824

EDITOR: Suzanne Venino

DESIGNER: Karen Groves: cover, book and map illustrations

PRODUCTION
MANAGER: Harlene Finn

PHOTOGRAPHS: © George Humphries, 1997. All rights reserved.
                 Northern Flicker and Eastern Chipmunk (page 67) © Bill Duyck, 1997.
                 All rights reserved.

TEXT: Essay © Harley E. Jolley, 1997. All rights reserved.
                 Natural science (pages 12, 20, 29, 40, 46, 55, 56, 60, 63, 67, 72 and 77)
                 © J. Dan Pittillo, 1997. All rights reserved.
                 Preface © George Humphries, 1997. All rights reserved.

PUBLISHER: WESTCLIFFE PUBLISHERS, INC.
                 2650 SOUTH ZUNI STREET
                 ENGLEWOOD, COLORADO 80110

PRINTED IN HONG KONG BY H & Y PRINTING LIMITED

*For more information about this and other fine books and calendars from
Westcliffe Publishers, please contact your local bookstore or contact us by
calling (303) 935-0900, faxing (303) 935-0903, or writing for a free color
catalogue.*

FIRST
FRONTISPIECE: *A hiking trail under a canopy of rhododendron in
                 Craggy Gardens, near mile marker 356 in North Carolina*

SECOND
FRONTISPIECE: *Maple trees in vibrant autumn color,
                 Irish Gap, near mile marker 37 in Virginia*

Cascading waters of Crabtree Falls, near the parkway, exit VA Highway 56 east in Virginia

PREFACE

While working on this book I had a lot of time to think about what the Blue Ridge Parkway means and how it has helped to shape my life. As I drove along the parkway and hiked its trails, a flood of rich memories from a lifetime of experiences came back to me.

For several summers in the mid-1950s my father worked as a ranger on the parkway in the Oteen District. One day in June 1955 my mother and I drove up to the Craggy Gardens Picnic Area to meet him for lunch. I was not quite five years old. The sky was Carolina blue—billowy cotton clouds rolled over the mountains and the rhododendron were bursting with blooms. We waited for my dad at the picnic area until a parkway worker told us that he was up at Craggy Visitor Center. He said, "You can drive up the parkway to the visitor center or you can hike Craggy Trail to get there." He pointed to a rhododendron canopied path that runs over a mile up to Craggy Shelter and down the other side to Craggy Visitor Center. Before the workman got the words out, I had taken out across the trail. It took my mother a few minutes to realize what I had done. She gave pursuit, afraid of rattlesnakes, but more frightened of what might happen to me. By the time she caught me I was already going down the other side of the mountain. We could look down at Craggy Center and see my dad. There was a huge black bear in a thicket. My dad stood between the bear and the hordes of tourists.

That episode is my first memory of the parkway. As I think back to that day I realize how blessed I have been. My parents taught me early and wisely to appreciate nature's wonders. I didn't know then as I ran that mountain path how that experience and other similar ones would shape my life.

George Humphries (on left) *with his parents Kathryn and Ralph ("Buff") and his cousin, Mac Powell*

The Blue Ridge Parkway is a magical road that runs 469 miles from Rockfish Gap, Virginia, to Cherokee, North Carolina. Riding the mountain crests and dipping into the valleys and gaps of the Southern Appalachians, it takes in some of the most beautiful scenery to be found anywhere in the world. For the first 355 miles through Virginia and part of North Carolina, the parkway follows the Blue Ridge Mountains. In the final 114 miles it skirts the southern end of the Black Mountains (providing access to Mount Mitchell, at 6,684 feet the highest peak east of the Mississippi River), then winds through the Craggies, the Pisgahs, and the Balsams.

The parkway also provides access to the James River Wilderness in Virginia and the Linville Gorge and Shining Rock Wildernesses in North Carolina. As the parkway weaves south from Shenandoah National Park to Great Smoky Mountains National Park, it ranges in elevation from 649 feet at the James River in Virginia to 6,053 feet at Richland Balsam in North Carolina. This remarkable variation in elevation encompasses a myriad of biodiversity. Forest types range from eastern hardwoods to spruce-fir on the highest peaks, with vegetation typical of Canada. Because of the variances in elevation and geology, this region supports more species of trees than the continent of Europe. Sassafras, fire cherry, sugar maple, buckeye, hemlock, white pine, red spruce, sweetgum, blackgum, sourwood, dogwood, basswood, tulip trees, silver bells, red and black oaks are just a few of the species found along parkway boundaries. Thousands of flowering plants—including more than a hundred rare and endangered species—thrive within the parkway margins. Showy orchids, pink and yellow lady slippers, Dutchman's breeches, purple-fringed orchids, bird-foot violets, spiderwort, bearded tongue, wake robin, goat's beard, Jack-in-the-pulpit are but a tiny sampling of the species found here. Flowers begin blooming in February and continue into November. Because of the differences in elevation, you can see rhododendron bloom from mid-May to early July, depending on the year and where you are on the parkway. In short, the Blue Ridge Parkway runs through the heart of the

Southern Appalachians, which harbor more biodiversity than any place in the world, except for sub-tropical or tropical regions. Here, in the Southern Highlands, nature went wild! I have heard the old-timers say, "When God made these mountains He was smiling."

Climb up to Sharp's Top or Buzzard's Roost at Peaks of Otter and survey the panoramic view of the Virginia highlands and piedmont—a view that has awed hikers since the days of Thomas Jefferson. Look out from Thunder Ridge and open your eyes to the beauty all around you. Hike the Tanawha Trail on Grandfather Mountain in autumn when the huckleberries and sugar maples turn to flame. From Potato Knob in the Black Mountains, let your eyes scan the horizon south to the Asheville watershed and Mount Pisgah beyond and east over the Pinnacle to the vast stretches of the North Carolina piedmont. Drive the Pisgah Ledge, where the mountains roll back like mighty waves in what seems an endless sea of ridges—silhouette after silhouette fading into the distance until you wonder if they are real. Or merely stop and smell the wildflowers blooming along the roadside. As Henry David Thoreau wrote in Walden a long time ago: "We need the tonic of wildness . . . We can never have enough of nature . . . We must be refreshed by the sight of inexhaustible vigor, vast and titanic features." The Blue Ridge Parkway makes nature accessible to millions of people that travel this ribbon of highway each year.

Unfortunately, that is one of the major problems the parkway now faces—too many people. Are we loving it to death? The effects of the overuse of the trails as well as damage caused by unthinking people who hike off-trail are becoming increasingly detrimental. Another paramount challenge for the parkway is preservation of its spectacular vistas. Historically, the land that bounded the parkway was the most remote and often the least desired. Today that is changing drastically. There is tremendous economic pressure to develop private land holdings that parallel the parkway. Even development in the distance can mar the splendid panoramic views that have become the parkway's signature. In addition, it is becoming

evident that the parkway plays a significant role as a greenway that facilitates genetic exchange between Shenandoah and Great Smoky Mountains National Parks. Accelerated development here might have irreparable impact. More study is needed, but it is clear that the future biological and scenic integrity of the parkway and adjacent federal, state, and municipal lands will depend on our vigilance and stewardship of these precious resources.

Over forty years ago I scampered across Craggy Trail eager to explore the world before me. My life has come full circle now. My wife, Linda, and I have taken our children—Katie, Sean, and Weston—to many of the special places on the parkway that my parents shared with me. Just the other day we stood at Waterrock Knob and watched the fog sliding over the ridges and down into the valleys of Nantahala. Mystical! The magic I have witnessed along the Blue Ridge Parkway and the lessons I have learned here under the tutelage of nature go far beyond words or photography. Yet I hope the images in this book convey a sense of the wonders I have experienced, and that they stir people to appreciate the Blue Ridge Parkway with a renewed commitment and spirit.

Ironically, the summer I finished this book my son Weston was not quite five years old. Our family went up to the Craggy Gardens Picnic Area to have our photo made for the book. My best friend, John Tingle, accompanied us and took our picture. As the photo session ended, we were clowning around, playing king of the mountain. Then John shouted, "Look, George!" As I turned around, there went Weston up Craggy Trail!

—George Humphries

Photographer George Humphries and his family, (left to right) Katie, Weston, Sean, and Linda

West Fork of the Pigeon River breaks the hush of the winter woods,
Pisgah National Forest, near mile marker 424, exit NC Highway 215 in North Carolina

A number of events conspired to set the stage for the drama of the Blue Ridge Parkway. Two new national parks—Shenandoah National Park in Virginia and the Great Smoky Mountains National Park in Tennessee—needed a road to link them. Such a park-to-park road would not only promote tourism but would also create employment. Millions of people had been without work during the Great Depression. The unrelenting, nationwide economic depression of the 1930s wrought major social and political changes, personified by a president who was willing to defy centuries of traditional thinking that had adhered to the belief that it was the duty of family, church, and local political entities to provide for the welfare of the needy. Instead, President Franklin D. Roosevelt believed that the federal government could, and should, step into this role. The building of a road through Appalachia would "make work" for the unemployed and open up a remote area to the economic benefits of tourism.

The term "parkway" was reportedly first used in 1869 by famed landscape architect Frederick Law Olmstead in referring to a project in Riverside, Illinois. The concept of a parkway—a road through a parklike setting—achieved further recognition with the building of the Bronx River and the Westchester County Parkways in New York, both built as part of urban renewal programs begun in the early 1900s. By 1909, a North Carolinian named Joseph Hyde Pratt took the concept a step further. He secured a charter to construct a "leisure-travel-only" road that he called "The Crest of the Blue Ridge Highway." He began construction on the road, which would have run from Wytheville, Virginia, to near Atlanta, Georgia, but the onset of World War I brought an end to the project. Just outside of Washington, D.C., the first federally funded parkway, the George Washington Memorial Parkway, was completed in 1930 and proved so popular that it encouraged similar projects. The June 1933 passage of the highly innovative National Industrial Recovery Act authorized the construction of "park ways."

A MOST VISIONARY THING

"It will be a wonder way over which the tourist will ride comfortably in his car, while he is stirred by a view as exhilarating as the aviator might see from his plane."
—Senator Harry F. Byrd

9

As is often the case with programs involving many government agencies and political personalities, there are varying stories about the true authorship and conception of the Blue Ridge Parkway. It is generally believed that the federal road project came about during a September 1933 meeting of federal and state relief administrators in Richmond, Virginia. Historians are not sure who initiated the idea, but they are certain that Senator Harry F. Byrd, former governor of Virginia, emerged as the primary force in moving the concept into reality. Byrd's role in establishing Shenandoah National Park and its scenic road—the appropriately named "Skyline Drive," which would serve as a model for the parkway—filled him with enthusiasm for the idea. "It will be a wonder way over which the tourist will ride comfortably in his car," said Byrd, "while he is stirred by a view as exhilarating as the aviator might see from his plane."

Senator Byrd explored the idea with Secretary Ickes and President Roosevelt, and each expressed his support. Roosevelt even suggested that the parkway begin at the Canadian border and follow the Appalachian Mountains all the way to Georgia. Building on this support, Byrd sent telegrams to the governors of North Carolina, Tennessee, and Virginia in October 1933. The text of the telegram informed them of the likelihood that the federal government would construct a leisure-only road without obligation to them, that the three states would share approximately equal mileage, that a toll might be levied, and that the result would be "the greatest scenic road in the world." He solicited their cooperation, asking them to inform Secretary Ickes if they were interested. Each state immediately confirmed support, albeit North Carolina vigorously refused to entertain a toll road.

As news of the proposed highway quickly spread throughout the region, there ensued political and economic commotion of a degree unseen since the Civil War. The public's reaction ran the gamut from "It's about time we got a road!" to "It'll never fly!" In his book *The Blue Ridge Parkway Guide*, William G. Lord, the parkway's first naturalist, captured the amazement that the coming of the road elicited from local folk. "One

Pioneer homestead, Humpback Rocks, near mile marker 6 in Virginia

Administered by the National Park Service, the 469-mile-long Blue Ridge Parkway winds through the mountains, forests, and farmlands of Virginia and North Carolina. Started in the 1930s as a make-work project during the Great Depression, this leisure-travel-only road was built for "the pleasure and recreation of those who use it rather than for the business of life," as cited in a 1938 issue of the "Blue Ridge Parkway News." Connecting Shenandoah National Park in Virginia with the Great Smoky Mountains National Park in North Carolina, the parkway showcases the scenic beauty, history, and cultural heritage of the Southern Appalachians.

The Blue Ridge Parkway travels the heart of Southern Highlands, passing through six mountain ranges. It follows the Blue Ridge Mountains for 355 miles, then traverses the Black Mountains, Great Craggies, Pisgahs, Great Balsams, and Plott Balsams. The Appalachians formed about 300 million years ago when continental landmasses collided. The North American continent, which was then located south of the equator, slowly drifted northeasterly, eventually colliding with Africa and forcing a small subcontinent on top of the North American plate. Just how high these mountains rose is a continuing debate among geologists, but 10,000 to 15,000 feet is a conservative estimate. The northwest thrusting of this collision is still evident at the Peaks of Otter in Virginia and the Great Craggies in North Carolina.

Humpback Rocks, near mile marker 7 in Virginia

12

of them hard surface roads like they have below the mountains?" a mountain matriarch was quoted as asking. "Why, Lord have mercy, nobody a-living could put one of them through here!"

Others saw the deeper significance of such a road, as entrepreneurs, farmers, boosters, and politicians realized the economic opportunities involved. Everyone wanted it to run directly by their front door. Long-time rivals in tourism, Asheville, North Carolina, and Knoxville, Tennessee, were exuberant and boldly determined to be the parkway's gateway city. Secretary Ickes was swamped with route proposals. Few of the applicants knew what a "parkway" was, but they didn't care so long as it was routed in their favor. Many of the areas through which the road would likely pass lacked paved roads of any kind, hence the excitement about a federally funded highway. To cope with the inundation of pleas, Secretary Ickes called for public hearings. One was held in Baltimore, Maryland, in February 1934, and another in Washington, D.C., in September 1934.

For North Carolina and Tennessee those hearings provided an unprecedented economic opportunity. At stake: securing a decision that would ensure millions of tourist dollars annually. Each state used every available lobbying resource, its most eloquent and influential politicians, and the strongest possible evidence to support its proposed route. Virginia, luckily, had an easily definable route running south from Skyline Drive to the North Carolina border. It was the remainder of the route that was to be determined. North Carolina proposed a route from the Virginia border south through North Carolina to the Great Smokies by way of Mount Mitchell and Asheville. Presenting the case for North Carolina, R. Getty Browning adeptly argued that this route would be cheaper to build and would also access more varied topography and more beautiful scenery than the route proposed by Tennessee. Tennessee countered with the fatuous argument that three American presidents and five rivers had had the good sense to depart North Carolina for Tennessee.

Overleaf: *South Fork of the Tye River, George Washington National Forest, near mile marker 29 in Virginia*

Rhododendron (Rhododendron catawbiense) *in bloom along Otter Creek, near mile marker 57 in Virginia*

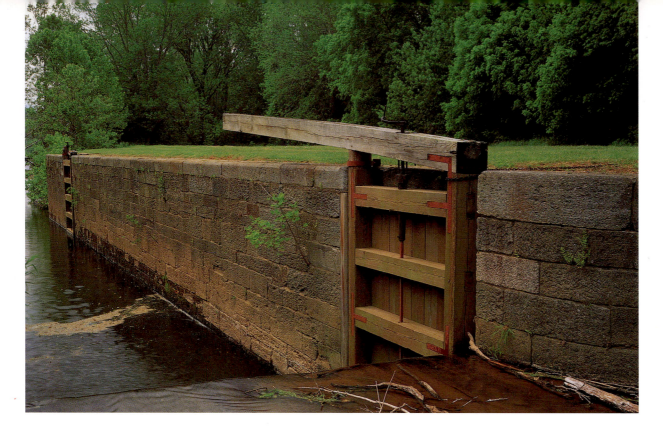

Restored lock, near mile marker 64 in Virginia. Built in the 1800s, the Kanawha Canal along the James River had nearly a hundred locks, making the river a major transportation corridor before the Civil War.

In a surprise move, Tennessee Senator McKellar demanded that Ickes abide by the recommendation made by his own special advisory committee, which, unbeknownst to North Carolina, supported Tennessee's proposal to leave the Blue Ridge at Linville, North Carolina, cross Roan Mountain, and run up the valley to the Smokies, making Gatlinburg, Tennessee, the gateway city. If accepted, that routing would have left Asheville with no parkway access and no tourist dollars from the proposed road. Ickes dismissed the final hearing without a decision, saying he would consider the evidence in depth and then announce a route.

That decision was announced two months later, favoring North Carolina and completely omitting Tennessee. Irate Tennesseans called

The James River—at 649 feet, the lowest elevation on the parkway— seen from the Trail of Trees, near mile marker 64 in Virginia

Ickes a traitor and asked President Roosevelt to reverse the decision. He did not and Ickes held firm, declaring that North Carolina did indeed have the more scenic and cheaper route, and that furthermore, Tennessee was already benefiting enormously from federal funding via the Tennessee Valley Authority's projects. The way was finally cleared for landscape architects, engineers, contractors, and thousands of relief workers to start construction of the parkway.

But first, certain administrative issues had to be solved. Which federal agency, for example, would have supervisory control? As Secretary of the Department of the Interior, Ickes had oversight of both the National Park Service and the Office of Public Works, and since the proposed road linked two national parks and was created as a make-work project, it fell under his auspices. He assigned the administrative duties to the National Park Service. Assigning the project to the Park Service carried important connotations: The parkway would have to be designed and constructed not as an ordinary road but as a route through a park—meaning there could be no commercial usage, no unsightly signs or chintzy roadside stands that would detract from the "park" experience. Instead, a deliberate, high-quality road and landscape design would enhance the beauty of every mile.

Just as critical was the choice of who would oversee the exact routing and design of the parkway. Almost from the beginning two highly talented landscape architects had served as advisory council for Ickes's route determination committee. Gilmore D. Clark and Stanley W. Abbott had both worked on the Westchester County Parkway system. Clark was considered by many to be the preeminent landscape architect of the time, and Abbott was his protegé. Clark recommended Abbott for the position, and on December 26, 1934, Abbott reported for duty as resident landscape architect.

With a solid background in landscape architecture from Cornell University, coupled with work experience at New York's Finger Lakes State Park and Westchester County Parkway, the twenty-six-year-old Abbott was well prepared for his challenging new task. He envisioned a

Flame azaleas (Rhododendron calendulaceum) *among the dense deciduous forests of the James River Valley, near mile marker 73 in Virginia*

The Blue Ridge Mountains take their name from the hazy mist that cloaks the range. Trees release hydrocarbons through leaf pores during photosynthesis; moisture attached to these hydrocarbon gases refracts the light, and the mountain ridges seem to fade into the distance in shades of blue. The high peaks of the Blue Ridge (Grandfather Mountain is the highest at 5,837 feet) wring moisture from clouds into the hollows below, which permeates down through the spongy soil. Water that collects in the rivers and streams on the east slope of the range flows to the Atlantic Ocean, while the west slope drains into the Gulf of Mexico, for the spine of the Blue Ridge forms the eastern Continental Divide.

20

Sunset, as seen from Thunder Ridge, near mile marker 74 in Virginia

linear park, a mere ribbon of road that would wind its sinuous way through rural valleys, national forests, and six mountain ranges. At numerous civic clubs and other gatherings he articulated his vision: "The parkway . . . has but one reason for existence, which is to please by revealing the charm and interest of the native American countryside . . . . The idea is to fit the parkway into the mountains as if nature had put it there." For the next eight years, until he went to off to war, Abbott would employ his skill and imagination to create a rural parkway that would not only showcase the natural beauty of the land but would also interpret the region's rich cultural history. Senator Byrd and others had dreamed up the concept of the parkway, but it was Abbott's ingenious talent that would convert that dream into reality. He was surely the fulfillment of the biblical prophecy: Your old men shall dream dreams and your young men shall see visions.

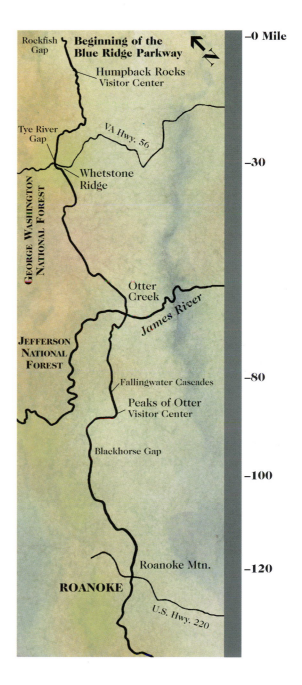

Rhododendron blossoms frame Fallingwater Cascades, near mile marker 83 in Virginia

efore Abbott could truly plan this pioneering rural parkway, certain administrative and political decisions had to be made. First, because North Carolina had so adamantly decried levying a toll, federal and state officials wisely adopted a compromise: If North Carolina and Virginia would acquire and donate the land, the federal government would design, construct, and maintain the parkway. By special legislation and right of eminent domain, each state slowly started acquiring and conveying the land. In turn, Congress appropriated four million dollars of federal emergency relief funds as start-up money.

The width of the road's right-of-way caused much debate. Traditional roads were built with a standard forty-foot right-of-way, but Abbott insisted on a minimum of two hundred feet for the parkway. Yet even that was quickly found inadequate to protect the road's scenic integrity. As the needs of a true parkway became more fully understood, an eight-hundred-foot right-of-way emerged, with considerable variances to accommodate numerous wayside parks.

In the meantime, Abbott had started inventorying the parkway's many historic and cultural resources. The corridor through which the road would run included, or was adjacent to, such classic examples of American architecture as Thomas Jefferson's Monticello, Moses H. Cone's Manor House, George W. Vanderbilt's Castle, Ed Mabry's gristmill, Caroline Brinegar's mountain cabin, and Polly Woods' Ordinary. The route also crossed or passed near the historic Howardsville Turnpike, the James River Canal, the Great Wagon Road, Daniel Boone's Trace, and the Drovers' Road. And all along the parkway's length, one constantly encountered reminders of bygone events, including Indian massacres, Revolutionary War campsites, and Civil War trenches, as well as the stories of fascinating personalities, such as Tom Dooley, made famous in song, and the life of Aunt Orelena Puckett, a mountain midwife.

Still, Abbott's task was a most daunting one—how to weave these rich historic and cultural resources into a leisure-oriented parkway

AMERICA'S
MAGNIFICENT
RURAL LIFE
MUSEUM

. . . .

"The parkway . . . has but

one reason for existence,

which is to please by

revealing the charm and

interest of the native

American countryside . . . "

—Stanley W. Abbott

23

Sharp's Top reflects in the lake at Peaks of Otter, near mile marker 86 in Virginia

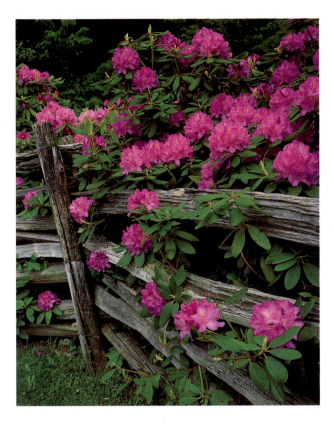

Split-rail fence crowded with native rhododendron, Peaks of Otter, near mile marker 86 in Virginia

through a mountainous rural landscape. He summoned two highly skilled landscape architects to help him. Hendrik E. Van Gelder was assigned to reconnoiter the Virginia route and Edward H. Abbuehl would scout North Carolina. It is somewhat ironic that Abbott (a northerner), Van Gelder (a Dutchman), and Abbuehl (who was from Kansas) should be teamed up to design a parkway through the heart of Southern Appalachia, but it was thanks to their vision that the parkway became the great scenic roadway and rural life museum that it is today.

With a rough sketch drawn up on his dining room table, Abbott began plotting which resources would be incorporated into the parkway. He included historic sites and buildings as well as museums and interpretive centers that would be constructed specifically as parkway attractions. He also planned picnic areas, campgrounds, hiking trails, and hundreds of scenic overlooks. Every mile would have one or more attraction to draw the visitor's attention. The ultimate draw would be a series of wayside parks. Recalling Frederick Law Olmstead's reference to the Boston park system as an "emerald necklace" of green parks, Abbott vowed that his wayside parks would be "like beads on a string—the rare gems in the necklace." Nineteen such parks were delineated on his planning map.

In pursuing their vision for this rural parkway it became readily apparent to the landscape team that there was no real role model to guide them. New York's famed Bronx River and Westchester County Parkways fell far short as role models since they were urban renewal projects designed to expedite commuter traffic, and hence could not be used as templates for the new rural parkway. Skyline Drive through Shenandoah National Park became a guide in "how not to." Its entire 105 miles never deviate from the ridge crests; whereas the basic idea of the new parkway was to incorporate a wide variety of vistas, ranging from valley floors to the crests of mile-high peaks. Moreover, Abbott was shocked by Shenandoah National Park's policy of razing and obliterating all evidence of human habitation. He was determined to preserve and incorporate into his parkway existing examples of rural culture, such as old logging railroads, homestead cabins, working gristmills, and other examples of mountain life and livelihoods.

So Abbott and his team of landscape architects developed their own set of guidelines. They would select a route that included as much scenic and topographical variety as possible. They would locate a right-of-way that encompassed "visual boundaries" that stretched to the horizons, making every effort to incorporate local farm and woodland scenes. They would marry the beauty of the natural landscape to the region's rich cultural heritage. They would establish numerous wayside recreation areas along the length of the parkway. And they would landscape extensively with native plants and trees to heal the scars of road building. These guidelines were adhered to by the National Park Service landscape architects, the Bureau of Public Roads engineers, highway right-of-way engineers for North Carolina and Virginia, plus the political agencies of those states and communities through which the road ran—a large-scale cooperative effort previously unprecedented in federal road building.

But as reconnaissance and planning proceeded, they hit a snag. The proposed southern terminus of the parkway ran through the town of Cherokee, North Carolina, the heart of the Cherokee Reservation. The Cherokee vigorously objected to the road on numerous grounds and a stalemate occurred. Rather than incur a poor public image and be accused of harassing the Cherokee, Ickes decided to bypass the reservation and end the parkway at the junction with the southern gateway to the Great Smoky Mountains National Park. Thus, milepost 469 lies in the park on the banks of the Oconaluftee River.

Because of the enormity of the project, coupled with the tedious process of land acquisition, and the sheer awesomeness of reconnoitering and selecting the best attractions, construction was delayed for two years—despite Secretary Ickes' frequent pleas to "Expedite! Expedite!" Finally, on September 11, 1935, a North Carolina construction firm, Nello Teer, made landmark history by scooping up the first shovel of

Maples in autumn color, Peaks of Otter, near mile marker 88 in Virginia

*Iron Mine Hollow Overlook,
above the Great Valley, near
mile marker 96 in Virginia*

dirt at a site designated "2-A-1" in North Carolina. A short time later, construction began in Virginia. At last, the parkway began fulfilling its make-work mission.

Captained by Abbott, his team of landscape architects continued with the primary reconnaissance. They located the center line and right-of-way, secured title to the land through the states, designed the road, let the bids, contracted the labor, and supervised construction. To further complicate the endeavor, the vast acreage incorporated into the master plan lay mostly in remote, unmapped, and largely inaccessible areas. Just getting to the designated work sites proved challenging.

One of the key elements in smoothing the way for the construction of the parkway was Abbott's charisma. In addition to overseeing the project, he was also the parkway's "ambassador of goodwill." He sought out local residents all along the route, befriended them, published newsletters briefing them on parkway events, and constantly assured them of the mutual benefits to be derived from their "joint project." So well did he accomplish this that the parkway still benefits from the goodwill he engendered.

From the very beginning the press had referred to the project as "The Shenandoah-Great Smoky Mountains National Parkway." In the rush to secure the best routing and to put the unemployed to work, that name was retained, even though it was a draftsman's nightmare. In 1936 it was proposed that the name be changed. Ickes was agreeable and sought nominations. He was besieged with proposals, including political paybacks like "The Ickes Parkway" and "The Franklin D. Roosevelt Parkway."

Ickes sought advice from the Division of Geographic Names, which indicated that "Appalachian Parkway" would be appropriate. He thought this was too broad, however, and declared the name "Blue Ridge Parkway" more fitting. In support of this, a congressional act in June 1936 officially

Over the many millions of years since the Southern Appalachians were formed, erosion has been the most significant geologic process to shape the land. Time, weather, and a warm, moist climate gradually wore down the sharp features of the mountains, with the tallest peaks now perhaps a third of their original height. As a mantle of soil covered the rock, plants eventually took root, holding the soil in place. Today these varied soils support the deciduous and evergreen forests that cloak the mountainsides. Soil deposited in the valleys below, locally known as coves, accumulated to a considerable thickness, and this is where the highest diversity of plant species is found. Soil that fanned out onto broad valley floors became fertile farmland.

designated it the Blue Ridge Parkway. That same act integrated the parkway into the national park system, where it remains today.

Other name changes followed. What was known as Negro Mountain in the 1930s is now Mount Jefferson; Bluffs Park has been renamed Doughton Park, honoring Congressman Robert L. Doughton, long-time parkway champion; and, fittingly, one of the most beautiful summits visible from the road now bears the name Browning Peak, as an appropriate tribute to the services rendered by R. Getty Browning.

Abbott field tested his design policies with the parkway, especially his philosophy of protecting the corridor from construction damage. "Carve and save rather than cut and gut" became and remained the ever-present catchphrase in guiding the construction. In a recent speech, E. Lynn Miller, Penn State's distinguished landscape architect, picturesquely described the process: "Like a surgeon, the landscape architect makes the incision to graft into nature a man-made device and carefully sews up the wound to restore the natural skin cover." The beauty of today's parkway defies the eye to discover either the incision or the graft, so adroitly precise were Abbott's operations.

Once construction was finally started, local men were employed by the thousands. The parkway was built in numerous sections that were then connected, with construction commencing first in areas where the right-of-way had been acquired and where people desperately needed to work. Two thousand men were working by the spring of 1936, with that number expected to rapidly increase. Over the years, many thousands of public relief workers labored on the parkway. A series of Civilian Conservation Corps (CCC) camps were scattered along the route, and later, during various wars, conscientious objectors were put to work on the parkway. In addition to blasting and building a road through the mountains, their role was to landscape the roadway to promote the area's scenic beauty. Even today, old-timers who labored on the road don't refer to the "parkway"; for them it is always "the scenic."

30

Sunrise over Peaks of Otter, seen from Blackhorse Gap, near mile marker 97 in Virginia

Bird-foot violets (Viola pedata) in bloom, Blackhorse Gap, near mile marker 99 in Virginia

Opposite: *Fog enshrouds black locusts and white pine trees, Rocky Knob Campground, near mile marker 169 in Virginia*

By the time World War II broke out, 316 miles of road, 43 viaducts, and 11 tunnels had been built. The war put an end to construction for the duration, and key administrators, including Abbott, went off to war. Construction slowly resumed after the war, but funding by a parsimonious Congress was so minimal that it took forty more years to complete construction, despite the constant prodding and politicking of North Carolina Congressman Robert L. Doughton.

One by one, the many road sections and wayside parks were completed until only one unit, popularly known as "the missing link," remained unfinished. From the early days of reconnaissance the Park Service had assumed that the route around Grandfather Mountain was firmly established, and construction of the parkway continued on a piecemeal basis, leaving that section to be finished last. But as the decades passed and a new owner acquired Grandfather Mountain, an extended, acrimonious battle ensued over the route around the mountain. Its owner contended that the mountain was so environmentally fragile that the Park Service's proposed high road would be as devastating as slashing the Mona Lisa with a dagger. The Park Service adamantly disagreed and refused the offered low road as being incompatible with park standards. A "You can't take the high road!" versus "We won't take the low road!" brouhaha ensued, lasting almost two decades.

After years of wrangling, reaching all the way to the halls of Congress, Park Service spokesmen masterminded a compromised middle route, utilizing state-of-the-art engineering to build an ingenious bridge. Dubbed the "Linn Cove Viaduct," it was built literally from the top down, in order to minimize environmental damage, with 153 precast concrete segments cantilevered into place. Completed in 1983, it spanned 1,243 feet and cost 7.9 million dollars. Nearly fifty years after the first parkway dirt was moved by a local company using an American-made Caterpillar machine, the Linn Cove Viaduct was built by a Swiss-French firm with equipment manufactured in Japan.

34

Flame azaleas, indigenous to the Central Appalachians, Rocky Knob, near mile marker 169 in Virginia

Flame azalea in riotous bloom, Rocky Knob, near mile marker 169 in Virginia

Autumn near Groundhog Mountain,
mile marker 188 in Virginia

Puckett Cabin, near mile marker 190 in Virginia

This mountain cabin was home to "Aunt" Orelena Puckett, who became a midwife at the age of 50 and delivered more than a thousand babies by the time she was 101. When winter weather made travel difficult, she pounded nails through the soles of her shoes and trudged through ice and snow to the expectant mother. In remote mountain communities, families depended on self-sufficiency and the help of neighbors to get by. Interpretive exhibits along the parkway illustrate many aspects of mountain life, from pioneer homesteads to the examples of mountain industry seen at Mabry Mill, where Ed Mabry and his wife, Lissie, once operated a gristmill, sawmill, and blacksmith shop.

37

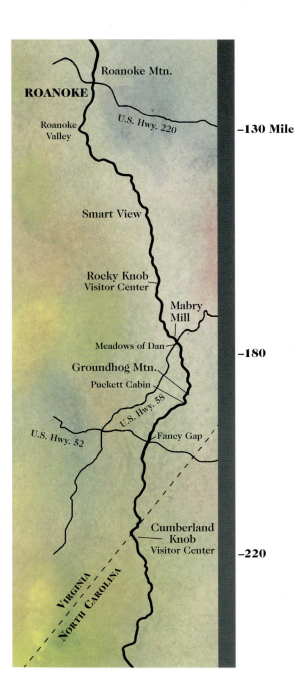

Roanoke Mtn.

ROANOKE

Roanoke Valley

U.S. Hwy. 220

–130 Mile

Smart View

Rocky Knob
Visitor Center

Mabry
Mill

Meadows of Dan

–180

Groundhog Mtn.

Puckett Cabin

U.S. Hwy. 58

U.S. Hwy. 52

Fancy Gap

Cumberland
Knob
Visitor Center

–220

VIRGINIA
NORTH CAROLINA

Forming a beautiful S-shaped, balconylike bridge, the Linn Cove Viaduct so aesthetically blended into the mountain, with minimal effect on the environment, that it has become an internationally renowned example of roadway engineering. The viaduct has garnered an impressive array of awards, including the highly prestigious Presidential Award for Design Excellence. Today landscape architects and road designers from around the world come to study the parkway, in particular the Linn Cove Viaduct.

Abbott, unfortunately, did not live to see the final crowning touch to his visionary project, but he undoubtedly would have appreciated the thought and care that went into it. Reminiscing about his parkway years, he paraphrased Kipling's poem "Envoy" in declaring: "I can't imagine a more creative job than locating the Blue Ridge Parkway, because you worked with a ten league canvas and a brush of comet's tail—moss and lichens collected on the shake roof of a Mabry Mill measured against huge panoramas that look out forever!"

View of Alligator Back in Doughton Park, near mile marker 243 in North Carolina

"Like a surgeon,
the landscape architect
makes the incision to graft
into nature a man-made
device and carefully sews up
the wound to restore the
natural skin cover."
—E. Lynn Miller

The Blue Ridge Parkway meanders through vast tracts of national forests: George Washington and Thomas Jefferson National Forests in Virginia, and Pisgah and Nantahala National Forests in North Carolina. Ninety percent of the trees that grow here were prominent some 65 million years ago. The sassafras, magnolias, oaks, hickories, walnuts, basswoods, and locusts seen along the parkway are in much the same composition as when the dinosaurs became extinct. Amazingly, many of these southern, or tropical, species survived the dramatic climatic changes experienced during periods of intermittent ice ages when glaciers formed as far south as the Ohio River. Now these southern trees are intermingled with northern varieties that took hold when temperatures dropped. Conifer forests of fir and spruce are evident at the cooler, higher elevations.

40

Jesse Brown's cabin, near mile marker 272 in North Carolina. Mountain families who came to hear circuit preachers at Cool Spring Baptist Church sometimes stayed here.

*Grandfather Mountain dressed in autumn colors, with Linn Cove Viaduct
skirting the mountainside, near mile marker 298 in North Carolina*

Grandfather Mountain dusted with snow, as seen from MacRae Meadows, just off the parkway near mile marker 302 in North Carolina

The Linville River flowing through the Linville Gorge Wilderness, access near mile marker 316 in North Carolina

44

Plunging waters of Linville Falls, with Fraser magnolia in bloom, Linville Gorge Wilderness

Opposite: *Scattering of beech leaves downstream from Linville Falls, Linville Gorge Wilderness*

Most of the rocks of the Blue Ridge Mountains are metamorphic in origin—compacted by heat and pressure over time to form a more dense, more highly crystalline rock. These metamorphic rocks, especially gneisses and schists, contain the same three minerals—quartz, feldspar, and mica—found in granite, an igneous rock formed by the solidification of volcanic magma. Granite and gneiss have the same general coloration (giving rise to the common misidentification of "taking gneiss for granite"), but while granite has an even mottling of gray and white, gneiss is more wavy and streaked, like a marbled cake.

46

Autumn sunrise over Tablerock, as seen from Wiseman's View, Linville Gorge Wilderness, exit at mile marker 318 in North Carolina

Eastern bluebird, one of numerous songbirds indigenous to the Southern Appalachians

A black bear cub, native to the Blue Ridge Mountains

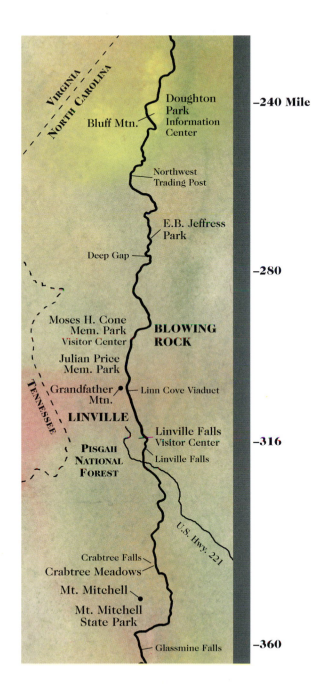

VIRGINIA
NORTH CAROLINA

Bluff Mtn.

Doughton Park Information Center

−240 Mile

Northwest Trading Post

E.B. Jeffress Park

Deep Gap

−280

Moses H. Cone Mem. Park
Visitor Center

BLOWING ROCK

Julian Price Mem. Park

TENNESSEE

Grandfather Mtn.

Linn Cove Viaduct

LINVILLE

Linville Falls Visitor Center

−316

PISGAH NATIONAL FOREST

Linville Falls

U.S. Hwy. 221

Crabtree Falls

Crabtree Meadows

Mt. Mitchell

Mt. Mitchell State Park

−360

Glassmine Falls

47

Large-flowered trillium (Trillium grandiflorum) *beneath a chestnut log,*
Chestoa View, near mile marker 319 in North Carolina

Forest floor carpeted with large-flowered trillium, McKinney Gap,
near mile marker 326 in North Carolina

Over the many decades that it took to complete the parkway, it has been recognized as an agent of transition. Among one of its many effects was bringing a better life to the people of rural Virginia and North Carolina. "It meant the difference between whether your family had a thirty-five dollar washing machine or had to wash clothes by hand," commented Bea Hensley, renowned craftsman and erudite mountain philosopher. "The parkway opened up a whole new life. I tell people that you could sell Henry Ford a Chevrolet if you had him on the parkway."

Indeed, one of the earliest transitions to accompany the parkway was an improved standard of living. The road provided employment and good wages to thousands of men whose families would have otherwise suffered. In the 1930s, standard wages in the mountains of Southern Appalachia, if a man could even find a job, were around ten cents an hour; laborers on the parkway started at about thirty-five cents an hour. From the beginning, the parkway provided a decent income for poor people forced to depend on subsistence farming to feed their families. Local men signed on as laborers, foremen, and even as rangers.

One of the most evident changes brought about by the parkway was opening up the region to tourists. Today the road and its wayside parks are major destinations for more than twenty-five million people each year, whereas half a century ago only a random hunter or herdsman frequented the higher elevations that are now so appealing to visitors. The parkway's lodges and restaurants have become attractions in themselves. Mabry Mill's buckwheat cakes bring steady droves of customers, as do the famed buffets at the Peaks of Otter Lodge, the trout dinners at Pisgah Inn, and the blackberry cobbler at the Bluff's Restaurant. Towns adjacent to the parkway have benefited from the coming of the parkway, as have the tourist-oriented cities of Asheville and Roanoke.

Changing recreation patterns and the influx of tourists have also proved a boost to the local arts and crafts economy. Gift outlets and arts

A DYNAMIC AGENT OF TRANSITION

. . . .

"It is a story of conservation, one of the great stories. It's a story of how things evolve!" — Secretary of the Interior, Stewart Udall

cooperatives along the parkway feature the handicrafts of regional artisans, from quilts and hand-carved toys to pottery, basketry, and blown glass. At the parkway's Folk Art Center near Asheville, the handiwork of craftspeople from nine states delights the gift-buying public.

But perhaps the most significant way in which the parkway has been an agent of transition is in the area of conservation. Some of the road's most popular and beautiful parks were but submarginal lands when they were purchased by the Resettlement Administration and transferred to the parkway in the 1930s. Through careful husbanding and skillful landscaping, these eyesores were converted into scenic gems. The parks at Rocky Knob and Cumberland Knob, recreational waysides visited by thousands annually, are excellent illustrations of this achievement.

In reality, the entire parkway was an exercise in conservation. For years, thousands of relief workers concentrated on projects aimed at improving the land and conserving its natural resources. Skilled in land and soil management, agronomists were employed by the parkway to teach neighboring farmers how to best use the land. The local farmers were provided with seeds and fertilizers and encouraged to emulate the land-use models established by the parkway. In doing so they gradually transformed eroded and depleted soils into a healthy, natural landscape. At a recent conference on linear parks, former Secretary of the Interior Stewart Udall declared that conservation was one of the parkway's greatest contributions. "It is a story of conservation, one of the great stories," said Udall. "It's a story of how things evolve!"

The story of the Blue Ridge Parkway continues to evolve. Many visitors are so enamored with the beauty of the region that they return to purchase land and build homes. The rustic log cabins of the 1930s have been replaced by expensive condominiums and second homes. Changing architectural styles can been seen all along the parkway corridor. Some counties abutting the road are reporting an annual turnover in land ownership as high as seventy-five percent. And with that comes rising real

estate prices. Fifty years ago, much of the parkway right-of-way was purchased for as little as four dollars an acre, with forty dollars considered exorbitant; now lots with parkway views sell for many thousands of dollars. Unfortunately some of the newcomers site their houses right in the middle of what were once pristine vistas. With these changes, the great American rural life museum may well become an endangered species.

In 1934 Senator Byrd estimated that the project would cost sixteen million dollars and take two years to complete. It took more than fifty years to finish the parkway, at a cost of 130 million dollars, not accounting for inflation. The many accolades it has received over the years still hold true. The Blue Ridge Parkway is still "the most visionary thing." It is still the "the world's pioneering rural parkway" and "America's magnificent rural life museum." And it has been, and will continue to be, "a dynamic agent of transition."

In 1959, at a dedication ceremony for a just completed section of the scenic highway, a full-blooded Cherokee led a prayer that beautifully described the Blue Ridge Parkway's remarkable role as an agent of change. "Where once there was only a buffalo trail, where Indian campfires once blazed . . . where once the red man and the white man fought . . . there is a road of peace and we are thankful."

—Harley E. Jolley

"The parkway opened up a whole new life."
— Bea Hensley, mountain philosopher

Crabtree Falls, near mile marker 340 in North Carolina

Autumn forest of oaks and maples, near mile marker 343 in North Carolina

Narrow ribbon of parkway on the ridge crests beneath Potato Knob in the Black Mountains, near mile marker 350 in North Carolina

Leaving the Blue Ridge Mountains, the parkway winds around the southern edge of the Black Mountains, where Mount Mitchell, at 6,684 feet, is the highest mountain east of the Mississippi. At this elevation the predominant trees are spruce and fir. The dark color of these evergreens seen from afar give the range its name. A short side trip into Mount Mitchell State Park illustrates the fragile nature of the spruce-fir forest. Many of the Fraser fir have died out due to an infestation of the balsam woolly adelgid, a small sap-sucking insect similar to the garden aphid. An epidemic outbreak in the 1950s killed most of the large trees.

The Great Craggies are nearly as high in elevation as the Black Mountains, but curiously this range is practically devoid of spruce and fir trees. Common here are yellow birch, beech trees, and heath balds—mountain folk call them "laurel hells." Heath balds are treeless areas with dense growths of flowering shrubs, most notably rhododendron and mountain laurel. In early to mid-June at Craggy Gardens, the magenta blossoms of Catawba rhododendron cover the high slopes of Craggy Dome, Craggy Pinnacle, and Craggy Knob—a showy display that is a favorite draw for tourists. Just below the viewing area atop Craggy Pinnacle is a protected habitat that supports a number of relict species from the last ice age: mountain club moss, single-flowered rush, and three-toothed cinquefoil, among others.

Sumac (Rhus glabra), *Goldenrod* (Solidago roanensis) *and Aster* (Aster curtisii) *add color along the parkway*

Overleaf: *Black-eyed Susans* (Rudbeckia hirta), *phlox* (Phlox carolina), *and coreopsis* (Coreopsis pubescens), *Craggy Gardens, near mile marker 368 in North Carolina*

Rhododendron give way to a clearing storm over the Walnut Mountains, near mile marker 361 in North Carolina

An amazing diversity of flowering plants grow in the highlands of the Southern Appalachians, brightening the surrounding forests and the roadsides of the Blue Ridge Parkway. A deep cover of rich soils combined with a hospitable climate and a wide variety of habitats—ranging in elevation from 649 to more than 6,000 feet above sea level—has resulted in this lush botanical garden. Watered by as much as 85 inches of rainfall per year, the region supports over 2,000 species of flowering plants, more than any comparably sized area in upland North America.

60

Crested Dwarf Iris (Iris cristata) *and Turkey-tail fungus, near mile marker 380 in North Carolina*

Sunrise over the French Broad River, near mile marker 393 in North Carolina

Opposite: *Fog fills the hollows of*
Mills River Valley, near mile
marker 404 in North Carolina

Autumn leaves frame Cold Mountain, in the vicinity of
Mount Pisgah, near mile marker 406 in North Carolina

After descending into the Asheville-Hendersonville basin and crossing the French Broad River, the Blue Ridge Parkway climbs toward Mt. Pisgah which has always been a local landmark. Nearby are the Pisgah Inn and the Mount Pisgah Campground, which is one of nineteen recreation areas strung along the length of the parkway. The campground has 70 sites each for tents and trailers. The 52-room inn is a destination in itself, set in the middle of a wilderness with miles of trails for exploring places such as Flat Laurel Gap, site of a 3,000-year-old heath community.

63

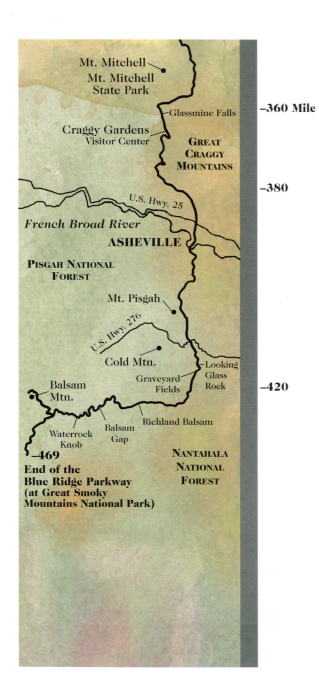

Mt. Mitchell

Mt. Mitchell
State Park

Glassmine Falls

—360 Mile

Craggy Gardens
Visitor Center

**GREAT
CRAGGY
MOUNTAINS**

—380

U.S. Hwy. 25

French Broad River

ASHEVILLE

**PISGAH NATIONAL
FOREST**

Mt. Pisgah

U.S. Hwy. 276

Cold Mtn.

Looking
Glass
Rock

Graveyard
Fields

—420

Balsam
Mtn.

Richland Balsam

Waterrock
Knob

Balsam
Gap

**NANTAHALA
NATIONAL
FOREST**

—469
**End of the
Blue Ridge Parkway
(at Great Smoky
Mountains National Park)**

64

*Growing to ten feet in height, Turk's-cap lilies (Lilium superbum)
bloom above Hominy Valley, near mile marker 409 in North Carolina*

Autumn leaves aswirl in Looking Glass Creek,
Pisgah National Forest, exit U.S. Highway 276 east,
near mile marker 412 in North Carolina

Frozen tableau of Looking Glass Falls,
near mile marker 412 in North Carolina

Eastern Chipmunk seen along the parkway

Northern Flicker feeding it's young in the cavity of a tree

Balancing on spindly legs, a young fawn appears among forest foliage

Numerous animal species are native to the Southern Appalachians. Black bear still roam the forests, as do white-tailed deer, bobcat and more familiar critters like groundhogs (known locally as "whistle pigs"), raccoons, rabbits, squirrels, and chipmunks. The elusive mountain lion is endangered and possibly extinct here; sightings are apparently of previously captive mountain lions that have been released into the wild. A variety of salamanders are indigenous to this moist region, as are frogs, and even the timber rattlesnake. Many species of songbirds are found here, along with golden eagles and other raptors, as the Southern Appalachians are a major migratory flyway. Even Monarch butterflies pass through on their annual migration from Canada to Mexico.

Autumn leaves carpet rock ledges along Looking Glass Creek, near mile marker 412 in North Carolina

Double rainbow arcs over Nobreeches Ridge, Shining Rock Wilderness, near mile marker 415 in North Carolina

Morning light sets the sky aglow, seen from Black Balsam Knob, near mile marker 420 in North Carolina

Autumn colors of Graveyard Fields frame the parkway and Looking Glass Rock, near mile marker 420 in North Carolina

Mixed deciduous and conifer forests are the dominant communities found along the Blue Ridge Parkway, although great tangles of health balds are seen among the high slopes and saddles, as are open areas known as grassy balds. This latter type of plant community is evident at Black Balsam Knob (near mile marker 420). Following intensive logging around the turn of the century, very hot fires burned over the area in 1925 and again in 1940. The basin of Graveyard Fields is now in plant succession, with scrubby shrubs and low trees in the lower parts and grassy balds on the ridges.

Sunset burnishes autumn grasses, as seen from Black Balsam Knob, just outside the Shining Rock Wilderness, near mile marker 420 in North Carolina

*Overlooking Courthouse Valley, Pisgah
National Forest, as seen from Beech Gap,
near mile marker 423 in North Carolina*

Autumn still life, Nantahala National Forest,
near mile marker 425 in North Carolina

Colors of sunset gild the low-lying clouds, Bear Pen Gap,
Nantahala National Forest, near mile marker 427 in North Carolina

Lone fir tree and skeletons silhouetted against a sunset sky, Richland Balsam—at 6,053 feet,
the highest point of the parkway—near mile marker 431 in North Carolina

The Great Balsams are named for the thick mantle of red spruce ("he-balsams") and Fraser fir ("she-balsams") that once covered its crest. Today only a few patches of spruce still stand on isolated high spots, as most of the trees have been logged or destroyed by forest fires. The parkway bisects the Plott Balsams on its final leg, traveling the last 12 miles through the Qualla Boundary, reservation of the Eastern Band of the Cherokee and ending at mile marker 469 on the banks of the Oconaluftee River.

*Stand of maples, near mile marker 442
in North Carolina*

Goldenrod brighten a hillside, Waterrock Knob, near mile marker 450 in North Carolina

View of Thomas Divide in Great Smoky Mountains National Park, near the end of the Blue Ridge Parkway